Snakes on the Hunt

ANACONDAS

Sebastian Avery

PowerKiDS
press

New York

Published in 2017 by The Rosen Publishing Group, Inc.
29 East 21st Street, New York, NY 10010

First Edition

Editor: Caitie McAneney
Book Design: Mickey Harmon

Photo Credits: Cover, pp. 4, 6, 10, 16, 20 (series logo) iLoveCoffeeDesign/Shutterstock.com; cover, pp. 1, 3, 4, 6, 8, 10, 12, 14, 16–18, 20, 22–24 (background) cla78/Shutterstock.com; cover (anaconda) Pete Oxford/Minden Pictures/Getty Images; p. 5 Steve Cooper/Science Source/Getty Images; p. 7 hin255/Shutterstock.com; p. 9 James Gerholdt/Science Source/Getty Images; p. 11 (main) JoeFotoSS/Shutterstock.com; p. 11 (map) ekler/Shutterstock.com; p. 13 Mark Carwardine/Photolibrary/Getty Images; p. 14 amskad/Shutterstock.com; p. 15 Paul Kennedy/Lonely Planet Images/Getty Images; p. 17 (anaconda) Vadim Petrakov/Shutterstock.com; p. 17 (caiman) Ammit Jack/Shutterstock.com; p. 17 (peccary) Ingrid Curry/Shutterstock.com; p. 17 (capybara) Ondrej Prosicky/Shutterstock.com; p. 19 Luciano Candisani/Minden Pictures/Getty Images; p. 21 guentermanaus/Shutterstock.com; p. 22 kovgabor/Shutterstock.com.

Cataloging-in-Publication Data

Names: Avery, Sebastian.
Title: Anacondas / Sebastian Avery.
Description: New York : PowerKids Press, 2017. | Series: Snakes on the hunt | Includes index.
Identifiers: ISBN 9781499421903 (pbk.) | ISBN 9781499421927 (library bound) | ISBN 9781499421910 (6 pack)
Subjects: LCSH: Anaconda-Juvenile literature.
Classification: LCC QL666.O63 A94 2017| DDC 597.96'7-dc23

Manufactured in the United States of America

CPSIA Compliance Information: Batch #BS16PK: For Further Information contact Rosen Publishing, New York, New York at 1-800-237-9932

Contents

Main Squeeze

Deep in the Amazon rain forest, a long, fat snake rests in the water of a slow-moving stream. Only its head pokes out of the water. It waits patiently until a deer approaches the stream to drink. Big mistake!

The green, or common, anaconda is the largest snake in the world by weight. It's big enough to capture deer and other large animals, such as wild pigs and jaguars. When an anaconda catches its **prey**, the snake gives the poor animal a hug so strong it can't breathe!

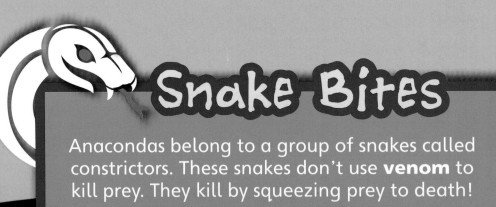

Snake Bites

Anacondas belong to a group of snakes called constrictors. These snakes don't use **venom** to kill prey. They kill by squeezing prey to death!

There are several kinds of anacondas, but this book will talk mainly about the green anaconda, shown here.

Looks like an Anaconda!

The green anaconda gets its name from its coloring. It can be green, grayish green, or brownish green. Most also have black spots. These colors allow the anaconda to hide from prey in its jungle surroundings.

As the heaviest snake in the world, the green anaconda can grow to more than 29 feet (8.8 m) long and weigh more than 550 pounds (249.5 kg)! Only the reticulated python is longer. The anaconda's size helps it catch many kinds of prey, from birds and fish to big cats.

Snake Bites

The green anaconda is an **apex** predator. That means it eats a lot of prey living in its surroundings, but it has few predators. The green anaconda's size makes it hard to kill and eat.

Female anacondas are usually much larger than males.

Baby Snakes

Most snakes lay eggs. However, mother anacondas give birth to 20 to 40 live young at one time. Larger snakes can have as many as 80 babies. The mother leaves her babies as soon as they're born. They're about 2 feet (0.6 m) long, and they quickly learn to hide and hunt.

Baby anacondas need to hide from or fight off larger animals. They grow rather quickly for three to four years. By that time, they have become **expert** hunters. They're also ready to start having babies.

Baby anacondas need to hide from frequent attacks from larger animals. Because of this, young anacondas are aggressive and bite often.

9

At Home in the Water

All kinds of anacondas, including the yellow anaconda, live in South American rain forests and wetlands. Anacondas are rather slow and clumsy on land, but they're expert swimmers.

Anacondas like to rest on logs near water. This allows them to warm up in the sun. They may also hide in slow-moving streams. This allows them to cool off. Everything but their eyes and **nostrils** is below water, making it very hard for prey to see them hiding.

Snake Bites

The scientific name for the green anaconda is *Eunectes murinus.* This is a combination of the Greek word for "good swimmer" and the Latin word for "of mice."

South America

green anaconda area

yellow anaconda area

The yellow anaconda, shown here, isn't as long as the green anaconda. It only grows to about 10 feet (3 m) long.

Stealthy Snakes

Anacondas spend most of their time lying around, waiting for food. They're often found hiding in shallow water or even mud. Anacondas usually hunt by ambushing their prey. That means they hide and wait for animals to wander by—then they strike! They can be found hanging in branches above rivers, which allows them to drop into the water and surprise prey.

Anacondas are most active in early evening when it's cooler. They may travel to find food or to find a **mate**.

Anacondas use **stealth** to ambush prey. Most animals don't see the snake until it's too late.

13

Snaky Senses

The anaconda's senses make it a great hunter. Its eyes and nostrils are positioned on top of its head. This allows it to sense prey while hidden mostly underwater. The anaconda uses its forked tongue to pick up scents around it. It also senses **vibrations** from nearby animals.

The anaconda has "pits" on its upper lip. These pits sense body heat from other animals. Altogether, these supersenses help the anaconda find and catch prey. They also help it find a mate.

tongue

Like all snakes, the anaconda has a special body part on the roof of its mouth called the Jacobson's **organ**. This body part recognizes scents collected by the forked tongue.

15

What's on the Menu?

Anacondas aren't that picky when it comes to selecting a meal. They eat smaller animals, such as fish, birds, turtles, and other snakes. They also catch and eat larger rain forest animals, such as deer, caimans, capybaras, peccaries, tapirs, and jaguars.

In addition to wild treats, anacondas are sometimes known to eat pets and livestock. They rarely attack people, but there are a few reports of it happening. People don't often go into the anacondas' home range, and anacondas prefer to remain in their wet **habitats**.

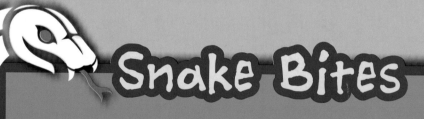

Snake Bites

Anacondas are also cannibals! That means they'll eat their own kind. Large female anacondas will eat smaller male anacondas.

Anacondas **digest** their food very slowly. This allows them to go for weeks or months without eating.

anaconda

capybara

caiman

Let's Eat!

Once prey comes close enough to a hiding anaconda, the snake strikes. It grabs the prey with its sharp fangs and hangs on tight. As the prey struggles, the anaconda wraps its long, strong body around it and squeezes. The squeezing cuts off the prey's blood and air supply, and it dies quickly.

Once the prey is dead, the anaconda stretches its jaw and opens its mouth really wide! It eats the prey head first and in one big gulp.

After an anaconda eats a big meal, you can see the shape of the animal inside its body! It takes awhile to digest a large animal completely.

19

Anaconda Threats

Anacondas might be apex predators, but they do have one deadly enemy—people. These two animals don't often cross paths. However, sometimes people hunt anacondas for their skin. Their body parts are sometimes sold as medicine. Some people catch them to sell them as pets.

One of the greatest dangers to anacondas is deforestation. People cut down trees and drain wetlands to make room for businesses and homes. That takes homes away from many kinds of animals, including anacondas.

Snake Bites

Other animals have been known to hunt green anacondas, including caimans, jaguars, and other green anacondas. However, it's rare for an adult anaconda to have a predator.

The Amazon rain forest loses millions of acres each year to unlawful logging and other human activities, such as soy farming and cattle ranching.

Protecting the Green Anaconda

What can people do to help protect green anacondas and their habitats? There are organizations that study and learn more about anacondas, and they sometimes accept **donations**. Never buy products made from anaconda skins or other body parts. You can also speak out against deforestation and habitat loss in the Amazon rain forest.

Green anacondas are some of the most successful predators in the world. But there's little reason for us to fear these huge snakes—we're not usually on the menu!

Glossary

apex: The top or highest point of something.

digest: To break down food inside the body so that the body can use it.

donation: A gift of money to a charity.

expert: Someone who has a special skill or knowledge.

habitat: The natural place where an animal or plant lives.

mate: One of two animals that come together to produce babies.

nostril: An opening through which an animal breathes.

organ: A body part that does a certain task.

prey: An animal hunted by other animals for food.

stealth: The act of doing something quietly and secretly.

venom: Something an animal makes in its body that can harm other animals.

vibration: A small, quick, back-and-forth movement.

Index

Websites

Due to the changing nature of Internet links, PowerKids Press has developed an online list of websites related to the subject of this book. This site is updated regularly. Please use this link to access the list: www.powerkidslinks.com/soth/ana